FELIX MENDELSSOHN-BARTHOLDY

CONCERTO

for

VIOLIN, PIANO

and

ORCHESTRA

D MINOR ✦ D-MOLL

mmo
3194

Suggestions for using this MMO edition

WE HAVE TRIED to create a product that will provide you an easy way to learn and perform this concerto with a complete accompaniment in the comfort of your own home. The following MMO features and techniques will help you maximize the effectiveness of the MMO practice and performance system:

Because it involves a fixed accompaniment performance, there is an inherent lack of flexibility in tempo. We have observed generally accepted tempi, but some may wish to perform at a different tempo, or to slow down or speed up the accompaniment for practice purposes. This album includes an alternate, slightly slower 'traditional tempo' version as well as a significantly slower 'practice tempo' version (see note below). However, for even more flexibility, you can purchase from MMO (or from other audio and electronics dealers) specialized CD players and recorders which allow variable speed while maintaining proper pitch. This is an indispensable tool for the serious musician and you may wish to look into purchasing this useful piece of equipment for full enjoyment of all your MMO editions.

Where the performer begins a piece solo or without an introduction from the accompanying instrument, we have provided a set of subtle taps before the movement as appropriate to help you enter with the proper tempo.

Chapter stops on your CD are conveniently located throughout the piece at the beginnings of practice sections, and are cross-referenced in the score. This should help you quickly find a desired place in the music as you learn the piece.

Chapter stops have also been placed at orchestra entrances (e.g., after cadenzas) so that, with the help of a second person, it is possible to perform a seamless version of the concerto alongside your MMO CD accompaniment. While we have allotted what is generally considered an average amount of time for a cadenza, each performer will have a different interpretation and observe individual tempi. Your personal rendition may preclude a perfect "fit" within the space provided. Therefore, by having a second person press the pause ‖ button on your CD player after the start of each cadenza, followed by the next track ▶▶ button, your CD will be cued to the orchestra's re-entry. When you as soloist are at the end of the cadenza or other solo passage, the second person can press the play ▶ (or pause ‖ button) on the CD remote to allow a synchronized orchestra re-entry.

We want to provide you with the most useful practice and performance accompaniments possible. If you have any suggestions for improving the MMO system, please feel free to contact us. You can reach us by e-mail at *info@musicminusone.com*.

About the 'practice tempo' version

AS AN ALTERNATIVE to the more virtuosic tempi observed in the standard MMO complete and accompaniment versions heard on this album, we have included a second, slow-tempo accompaniment version of the faster outer movements of the concerto. This will allow you to begin at a comfortably reduced speed until fingerings and technique are more firmly in grasp, at which time the full-speed (or 'traditional' tempo) version can be substituted.

CONTENTS

CONCERTO

for VIOLIN, PANO and STRING ORCHESTRA
D MINOR 🎵 D-MOLL

Edited by
Mario Hossen (Violin) and
Adrian Oetiker (Piano)

Felix Mendelssohn-Bartholdy
(1809-1847)

6

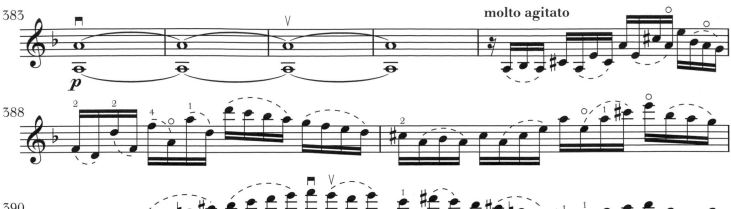

molto agitato

dolce

riten.

(dolce)

M CADENZA

468

471

476

481

485

488

491

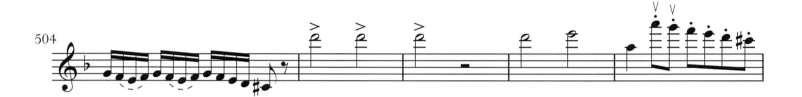

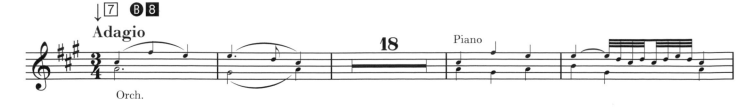

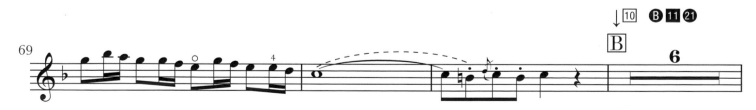

Piano

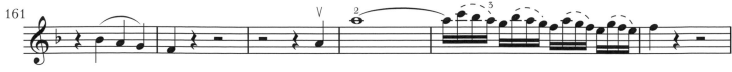

MUSIC MINUS ONE
50 Executive Boulevard
Elmsford, New York 10523-1325
800.669.7464 U.S. ← 914.592.1188 International

www.musicminusone.com
mmogroup@musicminusone.com

MMO 3194   Pub. No. 0960   Printed in USA